My First

Sticker Activity Book

This book belongs to

....

....

First published in 2015 by Scholastic Children's Books
Euston House, 24 Eversholt Street, London NW1 1DB
A division of Scholastic Ltd
www.scholastic.co.uk
Associated companies worldwide

Text copyright © 2015 Scholastic
Children's Books
Illustrations copyright © 2015 Jannie Ho

978 1407 14761 1

Printed in Malaysia
1 3 5 7 9 10 8 6 4 2

SCHOLASTIC

How many?

Count the objects and then use the stickers to put the correct number in each box.

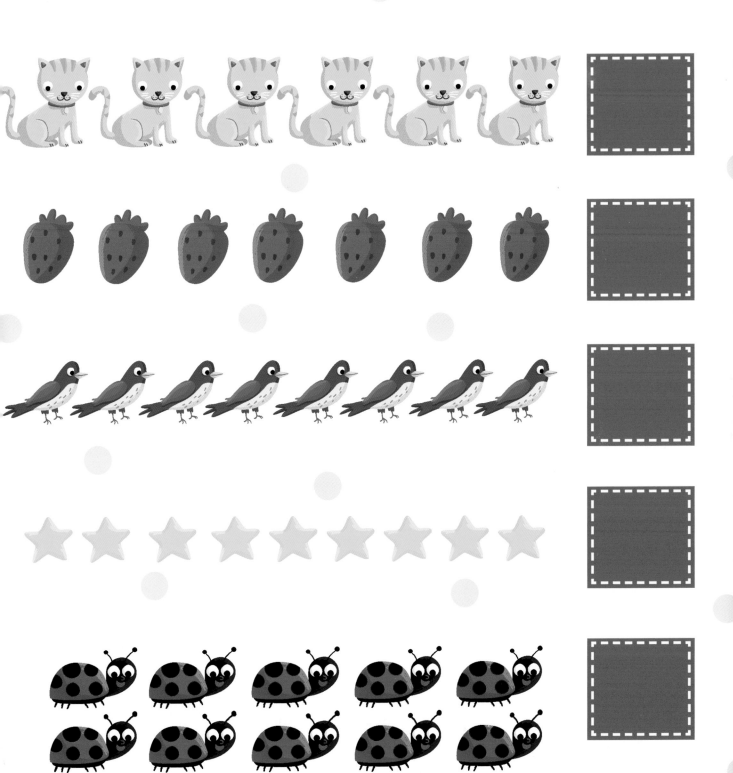

Let's write!

Follow the dotted lines to practise writing numbers 1 to 10.

On safari

Can you see 1 big elephant?
How many trees are there?
Add 1 stripy zebra to the picture.

2 Let's go!

Can you count 2 vans?
Put 2 cars on the road.

3 Picnic time

How many sandwiches can you see? Count the cupcakes. Put 3 apples on the empty plate.

4 Tweet, tweet!

How many eggs are in the nest?
Add 4 little birds to the tree.

5 Party time!

Can you count 5 presents?
Stick 5 bright balloons on the picture.

Use these stickers where you like

6 At the seaside

How many boats are sailing in the sea?
Count the clouds in the sky.
Put 6 shells in the sand.

7 On the farm

Count the hens in the farmyard.
Add **7** chicks to the picture.

8 In the garden

How many pretty flowers can you spot?
Can you count 8 buzzing bees?
Add 8 ladybirds to the garden.

9 Woof! Woof!

Can you count 9 dogs in the park?
Give each dog a ball.

10 Under the sea

How many crabs can you see on the seabed?
Add 10 colourful fish to the sea.

Matching pairs

Can you match the number to the right picture?

1

2

3

4

5